Merry Christmas

by Jenny Dooley & Chris Bates

Stage 1 Pupil's Book

D1574495

Express Publishing

Published by Express Publishing

Liberty House, New Greenham Park, Newbury,
Berkshire RG19 6HW
Tel.: (0044) 1635 817 363
Fax: (0044) 1635 817 463
e-mail: inquiries@expresspublishing.co.uk
http://www.expresspublishing.co.uk

First published in 2002

Published in this edition 2007

Made in EU

ISBN 978-1-84325-685-4

CONTENTS

Merry Christmas, Scene 1 .... p.   4

Song: Christmas Is Coming .... p. 10

Merry Christmas, Scene 2 .... p. 12

Song: It's Christmas Time .... p. 18

Merry Christmas, Scene 3 .... p. 20

Song: Get Ready .... p. 26

Merry Christmas, Scene 4 .... p. 28

Song: We Wish You A Merry Christmas .... p. 34

Activities .... p. 36

Now, let's act it out! .... p. 49

Word List .... p. 55

It's Christmas time at the North Pole.
It's snowing outside and it's very cold.
In Santa's workshop the elves are busy.
But it's Christmas time, so they're very happy!

snowing

workshop

busy

elves

4

a door

a postman

a bag   big   heavy

7

a list   letters   the world

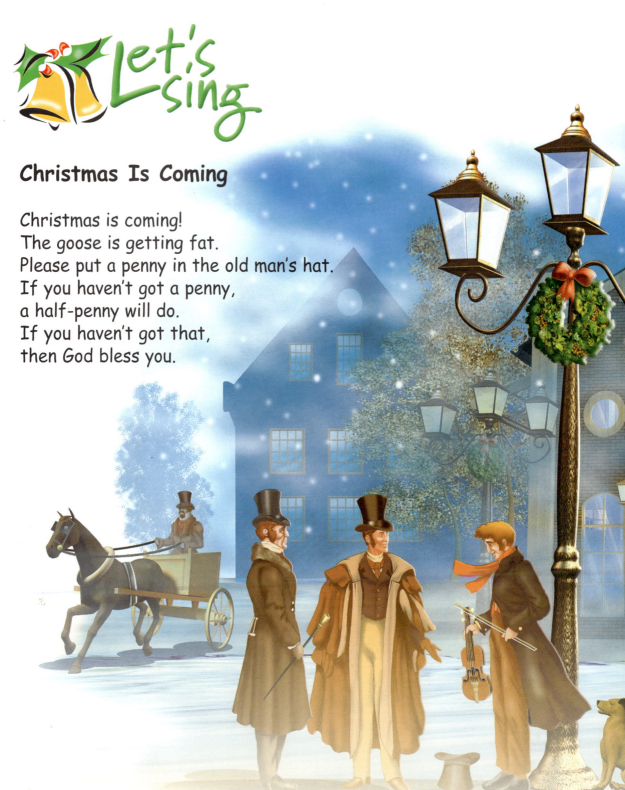

Let's sing

Christmas Is Coming

Christmas is coming!
The goose is getting fat.
Please put a penny in the old man's hat.
If you haven't got a penny,
a half-penny will do.
If you haven't got that,
then God bless you.

The presents are ready - it's Christmas Eve!
Now it's time for Santa to leave!

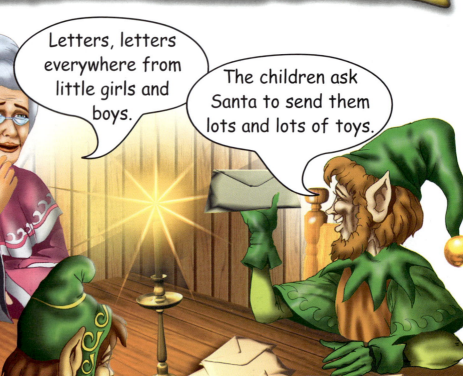

Letters, letters everywhere from little girls and boys.

The children ask Santa to send them lots and lots of toys.

presents

children

toys

Santa Claus

13

a doll

a teddy

15

happy

fly

a sleigh

Activities C-D

17

It's Christmas Time

It's Christmas time!
It's Christmas time!
Giving-away-the-presents time.
One for you and one for me.
Wrap them up and under the tree!

It's Christmas time!
It's Christmas time!
Laughing-and-singing-and-happy time.
Here's a bike and there's a ball.
Wrap them up and give them all!

19

Santa's reindeer are waiting outside.
They're getting ready to fly.

Hello, Santa.
Here's your sleigh!

Well done, reindeer!
Let's fly away!

reindeer

21

a nose

glow

22

23

Get Ready

Get ready! Get ready!
It's time to go!
Get ready! Get ready!
We mustn't be slow!
The sky is dark. The sack is full.
Get ready! Get ready,
the sleigh to pull.

Get ready! Get ready!
We're leaving tonight.
Get ready! Get ready!
It's Christmas Night.
The moon is up. The stars are bright,
Get ready! Get ready,
this Christmas Eve night.

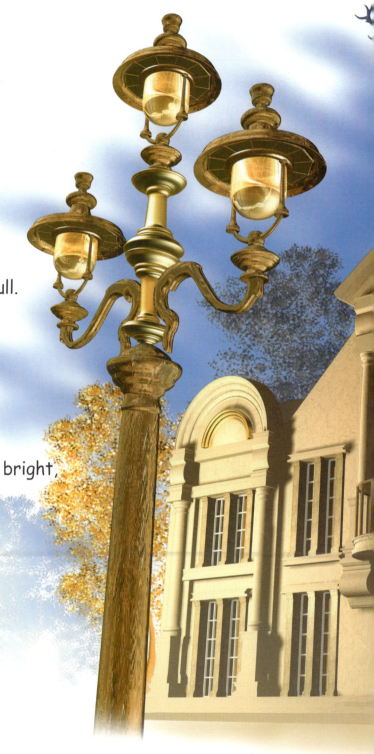

Santa's in the city now.
At John and Mary's house.
The children are sleeping in their beds,
with two small angels overhead!

Quiet, Santa!
Watch your step!
John and Mary are
both in bed!

a city   sleep   angels

28

29

31

milk   cookies

32

We Wish You A Merry Christmas

We wish you a Merry Christmas,
We wish you a Merry Christmas,
We wish you a Merry Christmas,
And a Happy New Year!

Good tidings we bring,
To you and your kin,
We wish you a Merry Christmas,
And a Happy New Year!

We wish you a Merry Christmas,
We wish you a Merry Christmas,
We wish you a Merry Christmas,
And a Happy New Year!

Activities for pages 4-9

A Look and write.

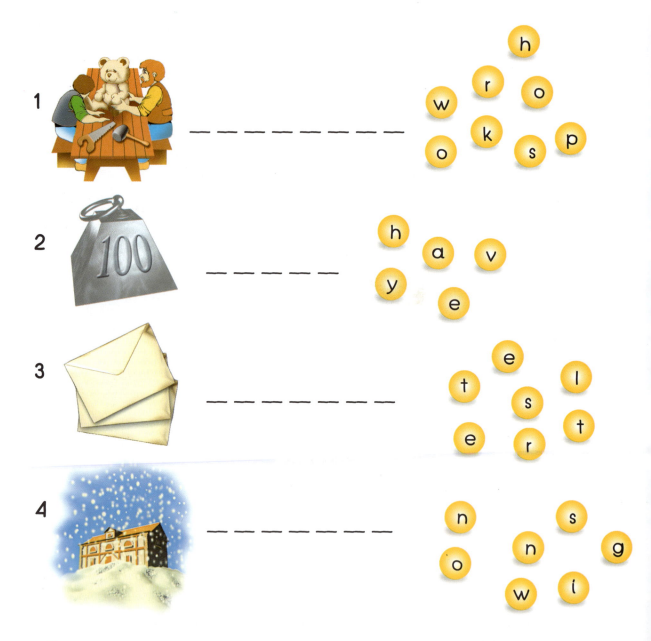

1 _ _ _ _ _ _ _ _

2 _ _ _ _ _

3 _ _ _ _ _ _

4 _ _ _ _ _ _ _

B Read and colour.

1 The elves are green.
2 The bag is red.
3 The world is blue.

4 The door is brown.
5 The list is yellow.

Activities for pages 12-17

C What's the word?

The secret word is...

_ _ _ _ _ _ _ _ !

D Look, read and write Yes or No.

1 Santa has got a teddy in his hands. ....No....

2 The teddy is green. ....

3 There are three elves in the picture. ....

4 The elves are reading letters. ....

5 The doll has got a red dress. ....

Activities for pages 20-25

E Look at the alphabet key and write the words.

A B C D E F G H I J K L M

N O P Q R S T U V W X Y Z

0 n o s e

1 _ _ _ _ _ _ _

2 _ _ _ _ _ _

3 _ _ _ _

4 _ _ _ _ _

5 _ _ _ _ _ _ _ _ _

40

F What do you want for Christmas? Write a list.

train

shoes

teddy

clown

List

jigsaw
puzzle

car

robot

ball

doll

bike

skateboard

G Read and draw lines.

snowing

Santa Claus

elves

reindeer

presents

workshop

sleigh

H Look and write.

heavy   happy   busy   snowing

It's ....heavy.......... .   It's ....   He's....................... .   They're................ .

 for pages 28-33

I Read and (circle).

J Read, look and write.

Dear [Santa icon] Santa,

Hello! My name's Ann. I want to come and see you at

your [workshop icon] ...., but it's [snow icon] .... a lot. Mum

says you've got nine beautiful [reindeer icon] ....,

and a big [sleigh icon] .... She says that

[elf icon] .... help you make all the [toy horse icon] .... Is it all true?

Love,
Ann

K Look, read and write Yes or No.

0 It is Christmas.   ....Yes....

1 Everybody is sleeping in Santa's workshop.   ....

2 A woman comes to the door.   ....

3 The postman brings letters.   ....

4 The teddy is for Mary.   ....

5 Rudolph has got a green nose.   ....

Activities for the whole story

L   Write sentences to show the differences between pictures A and B.

0   In picture A there is an angel, but in picture B there is a plane.

1   ....

....

2   ....

....

3   ....

....

4   ....

....

5   ....

....

6   ....

....

Colour the picture using the numbers to help you.

1 – red
2 – blue
3 – pink
4 – green
5 – yellow
6 – brown

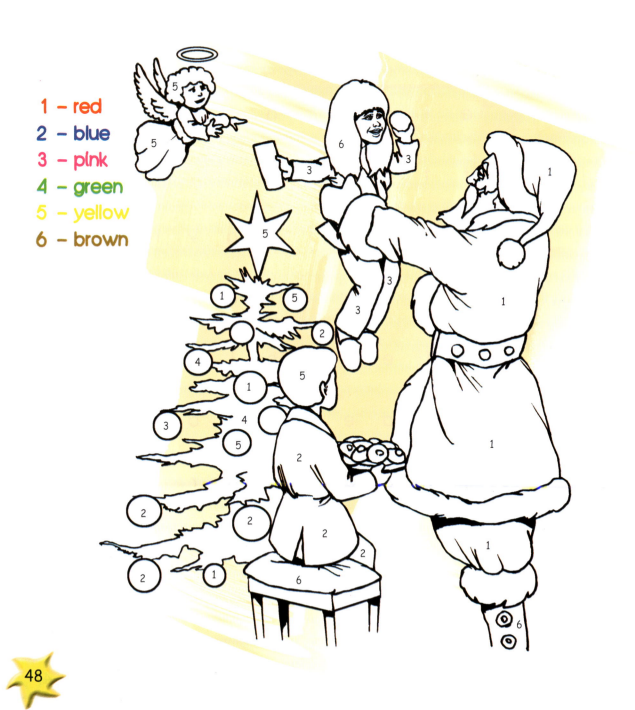

▶ Now, let's act it out!

Actors:

Santa Claus	Chief Elf	Peter, the postman
Mrs Claus	Elf 1	Rudolph
John	Elf 2	Vixen
Mary	Elf 3	7 Reindeer

Narrator: A student dressed as an elf or the teacher.

Scene 1

Narrator: It's Christmas time at the North Pole. It's snowing outside and it's very cold. In Santa's workshop the elves are busy. But it's Christmas time, so they're very happy!

Chief Elf: Hurry up! Hurry up! Christmas is coming!

Elf 1: Christmas is coming! Christmas is near!

Elf 3: Christmas is coming!

Elf 2: Everyone cheer! Who's at the door? Who can it be?

Elf 3: Who's at the door? Open and see!

Mrs Claus: It's Peter, the postman! Please come in!

Peter: Hello everybody!

Chief Elf: Hi, Peter! Come in!

Peter: Here you are! This bag's for you.

Mrs Claus: It's very big!

Chief Elf: And heavy, too!

Peter: It's full of letters from around the world.
From every little boy and girl!

Chief Elf: Christmas lists for Santa Claus!

Elf 2: From all the little girls and boys!

Peter: Well, Merry Christmas everyone!
I hope you have lots of fun!

Chief Elf: A Merry Christmas to you, too!

Elf 2: Goodbye, Peter. See you soon!

Song: Christmas Is Coming

Christmas is coming!
The goose is getting fat.
Please put a penny in the old man's hat.
If you haven't got a penny,
a half-penny will do.
If you haven't got that,
then God bless you.

50

Scene 2

Narrator:	The presents are ready – it's Christmas Eve! Now it's time for Santa to leave!
Mrs Claus:	Letters, letters everywhere from little girls and boys.
Chief Elf:	The children ask Santa to send them lots and lots of toys.
Santa:	Merry Christmas! Ho, ho, ho! It's nearly time for me to go!
Chief Elf:	It's nearly time, Santa Claus.
Elf 2:	To visit all the girls and boys.
Santa:	Lots and lots of lovely presents!
Chief Elf:	They're ready, Santa.
Santa:	Oh, thank heavens!
Elf 3:	A doll for Mary, a teddy for John.
Santa:	There's a present here for everyone! Happy children, everywhere.
Elf 2:	Time to go, Santa. Please take care!
Santa:	Time to fly!
Elf 1:	Everything's ready so, goodbye!
Chief Elf:	Away you go!
Elf 3:	On your sleigh over the snow!

Song: It's Christmas Time

It's Christmas time! It's Christmas time!
Giving-away-the-presents time.
One for you and one for me.
Wrap them up and under the tree!

It's Christmas time! It's Christmas time!
Laughing-and-singing-and-happy time.
Here's a bike and there's a ball.
Wrap them up and give them all!

Scene 3

Narrator: Santa's reindeer are waiting outside.
They're getting ready to fly.

Rudolph: Hello, Santa. Here's your sleigh!

Santa: Well done, reindeer! Let's fly away!
Here's Comet, here's Cupid.
Here's Dasher and Vixen.

Vixen: Here's Dancer and Prancer.
Here's Donner and Blitzen!

Santa: And what about Rudolph?
Are you ready to go?

Rudolph: One minute, Santa.
Let me make my nose glow!
We're ready to go, so hold on tight!

Santa: Rudolph, your nose is so bright tonight!
Don't worry, children. We're on our way.

Vixen: We'll be there for Christmas Day!

Santa: Christmas magic, Christmas fun!
Merry Christmas, everyone!

**Song : Get
Ready**

Get ready! Get ready! It's time to go!
Get ready! Get ready! We mustn't be slow!
The sky is dark. The sack is full.
Get ready! Get ready, the sleigh to pull.

Get ready! Get ready! We're leaving tonight.
Get ready! Get ready! It's Christmas Night.
The moon is up. The stars are bright.
Get ready! Get ready, this Christmas Eve night.

Scene 4

Narrator: Santa's in the city now.
At John and Mary's house.
The children are sleeping in their
beds with two small angels overhead!

Angel 1: Quiet, Santa! Watch your step!
John and Mary are both in bed!

John: Mary! Mary! What's that noise?

Mary: Maybe it's Santa with our toys!

Santa: Merry Christmas, Mary dear!

Mary: Santa! Wow! You're really here!

Santa: Merry Christmas, John, my boy!
You were good, so here's your toy!

John:	Thank you, Santa. Wow! A teddy!
	I will call him Little Eddy!
Mary:	Some milk and cookies, just for you.
Santa:	Now it's my turn to say thank you!
All:	Merry Christmas, everyone!
	We hope you have a lot of fun!

Song: We Wish You A Merry Christmas

Chorus: We wish you a Merry Christmas,
We wish you a Merry Christmas,
We wish you a Merry Christmas,
And a Happy New Year!

Good tidings we bring,
To you and your kin,
We wish you a Merry Christmas,
And a Happy New Year!

Repeat Chorus

▶ **Props**

Props	SCENE 1	SCENE 2	SCENE 3	SCENE 4
toys	✓			
tools	✓			
broom	✓			
mailbag and letters	✓	✓		
wrapped presents		✓		
doll and teddy		✓		✓
sack of presents			✓	✓
fairy dust			✓	
glass of milk and plate of cookies				✓

Word List

The words in colour are presented in the picture dictionary of the main story.

angels	every
around	everybody
away	everyone
bag	everything
bed	everywhere
big	fly
both	full
boy	fun
bright	get ready
busy	girl
cheer	glow
children	good
Christmas Eve	happy
Christmas time	heavy
city	hold tight
cold	hope
come in	Hurry up!
cookies	it's my turn
dear	leave
doll	letters
door	list
elves	little

Word List

lot
lovely
magic
maybe
Merry Christmas
milk
minute
near
nearly
noise
North Pole
nose
now
on our way
open
outside
overhead
please
postman
presents
quiet
ready
really
reindeer

Santa
Santa Claus
See you soon!
send
sleep
sleigh
small
snow
snowing
take care
teddy
Thank heavens!
time
tonight
toys
visit
wait
watch your step
Well done!
workshop
world
worry